ABANDONED SULPHUR
LOUISIANA

MIKE CORRELL

America Through Time is an imprint of Fonthill Media LLC
www.through-time.com
office@through-time.com

Published by Arcadia Publishing by arrangement with Fonthill Media LLC
For all general information, please contact Arcadia Publishing:
Telephone: 843-853-2070
Fax: 843-853-0044
E-mail: sales@arcadiapublishing.com
For customer service and orders:
Toll-Free 1-888-313-2665

www.arcadiapublishing.com

First published 2022

ISBN 978-1-63499-391-3

Typeset in Trade Gothic
Printed and bound in England

CONTENTS

ACKNOWLEDGMENTS

This book would not exist without the incredible people we met while staying in Sulphur, Louisiana, namely Harry Lee Louviere and Edna Veronie Bell, who we now consider family. This list further includes Taylor Bell Edwards, Grey Edwards, Camryn Louviere, Carsen Louviere, Candace Dawn, Jewel Flores, Samuel Louviere, and Scott Louviere. We love y'all! Last, but certainly not least, a big thank you to Dion Richard for showing us around the area.

INTRODUCTION

We discovered Sulphur, Louisiana, during the initiation period of full-time RV life. With our home sold and replaced by our RV, dubbed *The Steamboat*, we charted a southeasterly course from New Mexico, which eventually landed us in Sulphur. We arrived at a small Parish Park, Holbrook, having traveled nearly fourteen hours from Corpus Christi, Texas (our first stop), under the cover of night. Out of respect for the park host, who was likely asleep, we quietly parked in a roundabout near the back of the park.

When you first step from your comfort bubble into a new environment, all the sensory details are acutely apparent: the guttural sound of the toads, what locals call the *Ouaouarons* (pronounced "wa-wa-rons"), the crooning of some foreign night bird deep in a jungle of pine, palmetto, and cypress, the sweet scent of night-blooming flowers mixing with the loamy, earthen banks of the bayou, Spanish Moss draped like early Halloween decorations on the sagging arms of tree-giants, and the feel of thick, wet air filling your head and chest.

During the ensuing week of orientation, which included local foods such as boudin (pronounced "boo-dan") sausage, crawfish, jambalaya, and gumbo, as well as a driving tour with our park host Harry Lee Louviere, we explored Sulphur and the surrounding areas, including Moss Bluff and Westlake.

Edna Veronie Bell (left),
Harry Lee Louviere (right)

We came to discover a world rich with culture, history, and bayous. This flat swampy territory is riddled with waterways, snaking like veins and arteries between forests filled with crooked cypress trees. Sulphur is home to a Cajun populace, and unlike its more well-known southeastern counterpart, New Orleans, which is predominantly Creole, it was originally settled by Acadians. These French-Canadian settlers were excommunicated during the "Great Expulsion" of the French and Indian War and eventually colonized the Sulphur area.

Were it not for the mining boom of the mid-1800s Sulphur would likely have remained entirely Cajun and without modern infrastructure. As is often the case, however, the area became a hub of activity due to natural resources. After a rich sulfur deposit was discovered in the 1870s, industry interest drove railways into this unknown quadrant of America. Sulfur mining continued until the early 1900s, which was subsequently followed by an oil boom and the creation of water channels connecting the town of Sulphur to the Gulf of Mexico, twenty miles away. In the wake of this industrial revolution, many areas, both urban and rural, were left abandoned and in disrepair.

1

RURAL

Louisiana is well-known for famous abandoned locations, including mental hospitals, jails, and rice silos, but our tours, both with Mr. Harry and a local named Dion Richard (pronounced "ree-shard"), led us to corners not normally explored by the usual crowd of "urbex" enthusiasts. Mr. Harry's family has been in the area for a long time, and pieces of their lineage can be found throughout the surrounding rural areas. One such location was his grandfather's home. Mr. Harry stayed in his truck with a parting warning: stay out of the building and watch for an infestation of bees in the walls. Both warnings were heeded and became obvious as Joy and I worked the perimeter of the decaying home. The ceiling long ago collapsed, though the walls remain intact and all doors are securely locked. Glimpses through the grimy windows and web choked screens allowed views of a life left behind.

LOUVIERE FAMILY HOMESTEAD

Joy Correll

Joy Correll

Joy Correll

Joy Correll

Joy Correll

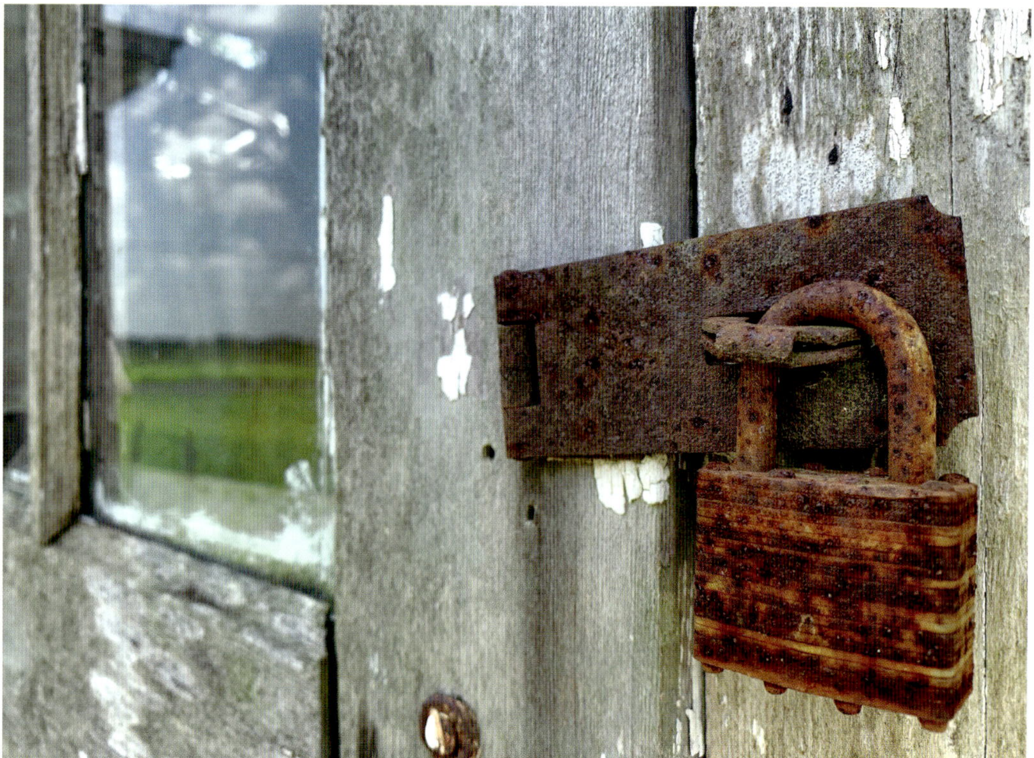

Joy Correll

Joy Correll

Joy Correll

Joy Correll

Joy Correll

Joy Correll

Not far from Mr. Harry's family homestead is a nearly abandoned cemetery, and we had the opportunity to tour its remains. Everything in Louisiana is flat, so I found myself lost in the expanse of crawfish fields, telephone lines, rice silos, and lonesome rural homes, and my ability to judge distance became compromised. Nevertheless, it seemed a long, bouncy ride on dirt roads before we arrived at Ardoin (pronounced "ard-wahn") Cove Cemetery, the rumbling truck engine often stirring pink-tinged Egrets from the roadside slews. The portion of the cemetery that we explored with Mr. Harry exists behind a short chain link fence that has a modest locked gate. Mr. Harry explained that a great deal more of the cemetery exists beyond the farthest reaches of the mowed area, but the graves have all been disturbed by water, namely yearly hurricanes, and are therefore off-limits. The remains of the undisturbed areas boast concrete vaults, unmarked brick-inlaid tombs, and headstones often bearing no indication of date, simply the person's name. Many of the older tombstones and markers honored people who were born in the early and mid-1800s. While a handful of the graves were newer, the vast majority were not only older but clearly in disrepair and suffering from neglect.

ARDOIN COVE CEMETERY

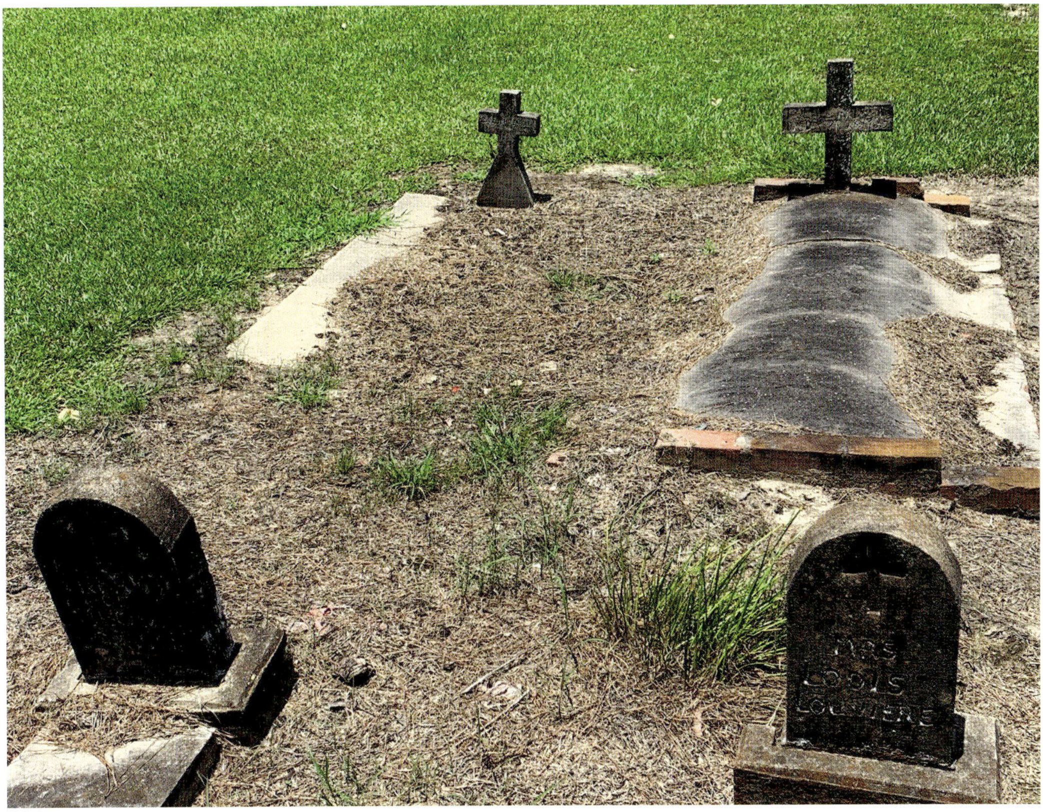

TOEFFEL ARDOIN
DIED SEPT 28 1925

Joy Correll

By His hand
made of God
Joy Correll

ETTIENE ARDOIN
SEPT 30 1851
MAY 19 1934

Joy Correll

Joy Correll

2

COMMERCIAL

On our way back to Holbrook, Mr. Harry made a side stop at an abandoned grocery store near a "Y"-shaped crossroads. During its glory days, the grocery store provided a necessary service for those inhabiting the area, and given that most residential homes exist on long stretches of remote dirt roads, I am quite sure it prospered in the bardo zone of Sulphur and Moss Bluff. A quick inspection of the exterior revealed several open entrances to the abandoned building, and not a single "no trespassing" sign, so we ventured into the depths. The wet floor was difficult to navigate and the musty smell of rot, tinged with ammonia, was sharp in my nose. It was evident that the building's current occupants were engaged in questionable activities, so while I wanted to explore and capture the dark beauty of this forgotten place, I did not care to stumble upon anyone living or deceased. Note: Green Acres Grocery has since been demolished.

GREEN ACRES GROCERY

While traveling the commercial districts with Mr. Harry, we scouted several locations worthy of investigation. On the following day, when we were on our own, we had a handful of abandoned structures to explore. Southwest Louisiana is different than many places, because it has both old abandoned structures, and newly abandoned structures. The heartbeat that drives this expansion and contraction, this push and pull of humanity, is oil. During a boom, people flow into the area and infrastructure is developed to support them. During a dry spell, people leave, businesses close, and empty tracts are left in the wake. Similarly, hurricanes dominate both the landscape and the people, often doing irreparable damage.

West End Carwash

D & C Appliances

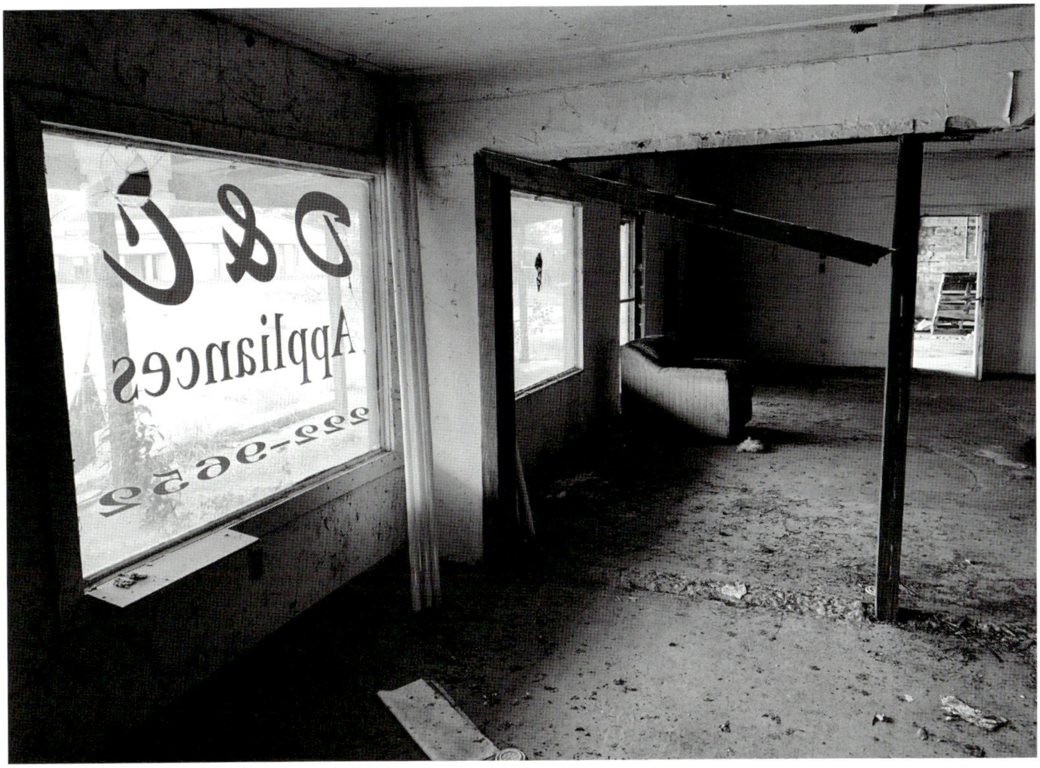

Numbe
World
Are you
for a

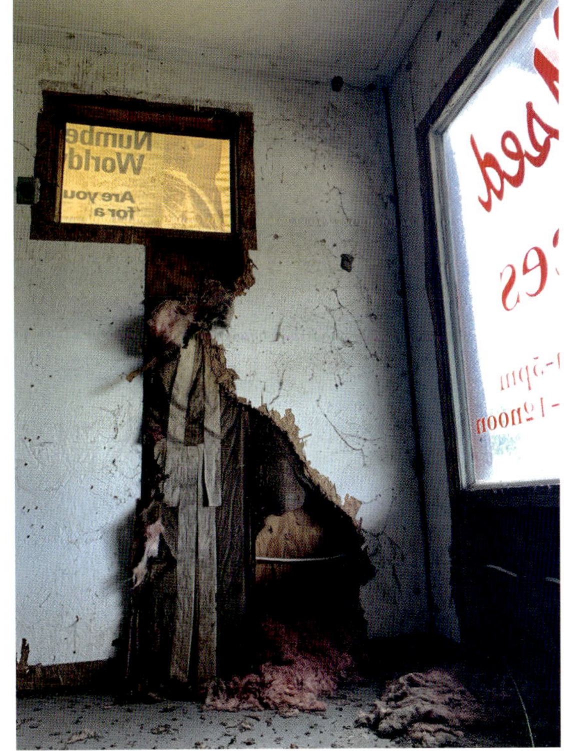

One of the things that has always attracted me to abandoned locations is the austere beauty of the neglected or forgotten. The textures, colors, shadows, and lines speak of a life once lived within the confines, and the absence is as empty as it is filled. I can feel the wheel of time turn within these places as nature takes back what was only borrowed, infiltrating the cracks and seams with the tendrils of her vine-fingers, while spray painting the surfaces with moss, mold, and dirt. There is a sense of danger in these places too, and the evidence of vandalism, vagrancy, and drug abuse often heralds the reminder that you are at risk. Indeed, danger can be attractive as well.

Unidentified Mechanic's Shop

3

INDUSTRIAL

During our two-week stay at Holbrook park, we had several "neighbors," all of them locals, who stayed for several days at a time. One of these neighbors was a man named Dion, and his family, much like Mr. Harry's, had inhabited the area for many generations, so he worked and lived locally. Dion is also a full-time RV enthusiast, though he lives in a "bumper pull" trailer, so when he takes a vacation, he pulls his home to a local parish park for a week or so. Like so many Sulphurites, Dion is gregarious, outspoken, and social, so when he invited us over for dinner with the phrase, "Come getchu a plate," it was less an invite and more of a command. During one of these meals, Dion hinted at a few places that he knew of, including an abandoned highway that once connected the city of Lake Charles to Westlake and Sulphur. This certainly piqued my interests, so I took Dion's tact and "invited" him to take me on a tour of the area the following day.

MIKE HOOKS ROAD (OLD U.S. 90)

STOP
AUTHORIZED
PERSONNEL ONLY

Joy Correll

Joy Correll

Joy Correll

Joy Correll

After spending over an hour with the dilapidated highway, Dion suggested that we roll a few miles down the road and shoot photography of an abandoned parking garage that, according to Dion, was used along with the adjacent parking lot for evacuees during one of the many hurricanes. The parking garage has since been decommissioned and now lies behind a rickety, six foot tall, chain link fence. Signs clearly state the criminal repercussions for trespassing, so while the urge to breach the fence and explore the inner depths was great, we chose to remain outside.

Unidentified Parking Garage

Joy Correll

UNLAWFUL
TO UNLAWFULLY TAMPER
WITH OR TRESPASS
UPON A CONSTRUCTION
PROJECT
UP TO $1000 FINE OR
6 MONTHS IN JAIL
SECTION 13-37.3
LAKE CHARLES
CODE OF
ORDINANCES

Lo Fi Dream
Joy Correll

Joy Correll

4

RESIDENTIAL

There were locations along the route that Dion pointed out but did not want to stop at, so I marked them in my mind, and we visited them on a subsequent day. These locations allowed partial access with no signage, but it was also obvious that attempts had been made to secure the locations, so we did not enter the domiciles out of respect for the owners. I always find it curious to discover a home left as if in a state of interrupted daily life, with clothes still hanging like flaccid skins in a closet. Despite the rubble of personal effects, I can imagine someone sitting in their favorite chair, smoking an evening cigarette, or tinkering on their best friend's truck in the garage.

SULPHUR

Moss Bluff

One of the locations at the top of Dion's list was an abandoned house that he often drove by on the way to work. Given its proximity to his home, he opted to stay in a nearby parking lot, and I explored solo. The electric hum of cicadas, which was a low drone near the road, become an overwhelming vibration in the neck-deep brush that had taken back what was once a long driveway and front yard. By the time I reached the structure, beads of sweat were rolling off my lips and the tip of my nose, and my skin was covered in the slick of Louisiana humidity. The faded lime-colored building was, like so many other residential locations in the area, a snapshot out of time, as if the occupant had simply walked away one day. Blooms of mold seemed strung together by webs lacing the exterior—constellations marked by Mud dauber high-rises and sticky spider holes.

Abandoned residential homes are common in the area—often the casualties of severe damage from hurricanes—but what I find fascinating is the mettle of the Cajuns we encountered and befriended. They may lose their roof and be forced to abandon their home, but it is a near surety that they will remain in the same area, raising a family. There is great cultural pride in these resourceful people, and it is evidenced by the tenacity of those who face the power of Gulf hurricanes every year, and yet remain. It can also be seen in something as simple as a trailer with cupcakes painted upon it. Granted, the business was defunct, but the evidence of an effort to make something out of nothing exists nonetheless.

WESTLAKE

Joy Correll

Joy Correll

Joy Correll

Joy Correll

SULPHUR

SULPHUR

AFTERWORD

The ones that got away haunt me, because I can see them so clearly in my mind. Recently I saw a children's playground half-submerged in water. The reflection of the 1980s style, derelict slide, swing-set, and merry-go-round in the brackish waters was smooth, still, and immaculate. Inevitably the picture was taken, but only in the upstairs compartments of my brain-attic. I knew I would return to shoot the image later. Alas, there was no later!

We awoke at five in the morning to an intense downpour and lightning laser beams crashing around The Steamboat. We dressed for the worst and began battening down the hatches as three inches of water bled from the sky in an hour and a half. On the way out of the park, not long after, I thought longingly of the flooded and abandoned playground, which now belongs to the file: the ones that got away.

ABOUT THE AUTHOR

MIKE CORRELL, along with his wife, Joy Correll, is a full-time RV journalist and photographer. Correll is also a fine artist, inventor (MYSTERIAN all-in-one Oracle and Card Game), award-winning documentary filmmaker (*Chet Zar: I Like to Paint Monsters, The Many Faces of Homelessness, Labyrinth of Penumbra*), published author (*DY5TOPIA: A Field Guide to the Dark Universe of Chet Zar*), eleven-time successful crowdfunding project manager, and co-founder of the Dark Art Society. He graduated with a bachelor of arts from Fairhaven College at Western Washington University, where he pioneering a degree titled "Imaginative Moviemaking." His studies included screenwriting, film appreciation, video production, and fine arts. More about Correll here: https://www.patreon.com/EmailsFromInfinity